On Sam's Boat

by Rachel Dille • illustrated by Annie Lunsford

Harcourt

Orlando   Boston   Dallas   Chicago   San Diego

www.harcourtschool.com

I am Sam.

What is that mat?

Look at that mat.

What is that hat?

Look at that hat.

What is in the hat?

Look at that cat!